About Arachnids

Books in the ABOUT… series

About Arachnids

A Guide for Children

Cathryn Sill

Illustrated by John Sill

Ω

PEACHTREE
ATLANTA

For the One who created arachnids.

—*Genesis* 1:25

Published by
PEACHTREE PUBLISHERS
1700 Chattahoochee Avenue
Atlanta, Georgia 30318-2112
www.peachtree-online.com

Text © 2003 Cathryn P. Sill
Jacket and interior illustrations © 2003 John C. Sill

First trade paperback edition published 2006

Illustrations painted in watercolor on archival quality 100% rag watercolor paper
Text and titles set in Novarese from Adobe Systems

Manufactured in China

10 9 8 7 6 5 4 3 (hardcover)
10 9 8 7 6 5 4 3 2 1 (trade paperback)

Library of Congress Cataloging-in-Publication Data

Sill, Cathryn P., 1953-
  About arachnids / written by Cathryn P. Sill ; illustrated by John
Sill.-- 1st ed.
      p. cm.
Summary: An introduction to the physical characteristics, behavior, and
life cycle of arachnids.

ISBN 1-56145-038-3 (hardcover)
ISBN 1-56145-364-1 (trade paperback)

1. Arachnida--Juvenile literature. [1. Arachnids.] I. Sill, John, illus. II. Title.
QL452.2 .S55 2003
595.4--dc21   2002011739

About Arachnids

Arachnids have eight legs…

and two main body parts.

PLATE 2
Desert Tarantula

They have a skeleton on the outside
of their bodies.

PLATE 3
Crablike Spiny Orb Weaver

Most arachnids live on land.

PLATE 4
Giant Vinegaroon

Most arachnids are predators, hunting for and eating smaller animals.

PLATE 5
California Trapdoor Spider

Some have a poisonous bite that helps them eat their prey.

Others suck blood from larger animals.

PLATE 7
Eastern Wood Tick

Some use pincers and a stinger to catch food and protect themselves.

PLATE 8
Giant Desert Hairy Scorpion

Many arachnids spin silk to help them capture food.

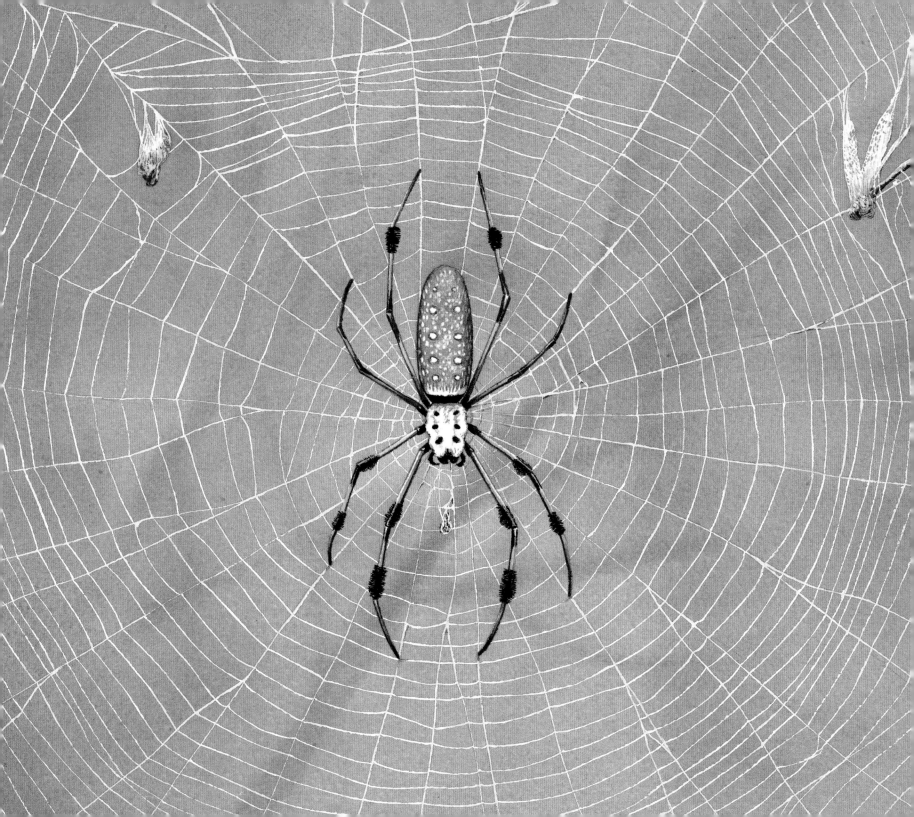

They may also use the silk to help them travel…

or protect their young.

PLATE 11
Nursery Web Spider

Some mother arachnids care for
their eggs or babies.

A few arachnids are too tiny to be easily seen.

Some arachnids may cause harm…

but most are helpful and should be protected.

Afterword

PLATE 1

Arachnids are a class of arthropods—animals with distinctly divided body parts, jointed legs, and a hard outer covering called an exoskeleton. Spiders, scorpions, ticks, mites, and harvestmen are arachnids. Harvestmen, often mistaken for spiders, are sometimes called daddy longlegs. The Brown Daddy Longlegs, like all harvestmen, is nocturnal (active at night). It eats small insects and decaying organic matter.

PLATE 2

The front part of an arachnid's body, where the four pairs of legs are attached, is called the cephalothorax. It contains the sense organs and the mouthparts. The back part, or abdomen, contains the heart and the reproductive system. The Desert Tarantula eats insects, lizards, and other small animals. Although this spider looks scary, its venom is no more poisonous than a bee sting.

PLATE 3

An arachnid's outside covering or exoskeleton protects it from attacks and keeps it from drying out. In order to grow, arachnids must periodically shed this hard body covering. The female Crablike Spiny Orb Weaver has an unusual exoskeleton: six pointed "spines" project from her abdomen. This spider spins a new web each night.

PLATE 4

Arachnids are found all over the world in almost every habitat. The Giant Vinegarone is a whip scorpion. There are nearly seventy species of vinegarones in the world, but the Giant Vinegarone is the only one that lives in North America. When threatened, this arachnid sprays an acid that smells like vinegar from the base of its tail.

PLATE 5

Spiders are very useful predators because they control insects by catching and eating them. The California Trapdoor Spider digs tunnels or burrows in the ground, which it covers with a hinged lid or trapdoor. As prey passes by, the spider rushes out to seize it and then drags it into the burrow.

PLATE 6

Many spiders have a bite that poisons their prey. They use sharp fangs to inject the animal with digestive juices. When these juices break down the tissue, the arachnids are able to suck up a meal. The Black Widow Spider is shy and will try to escape when threatened. Bites to humans, though poisonous, are rare. This spider is called "widow" because the female sometimes eats the male.

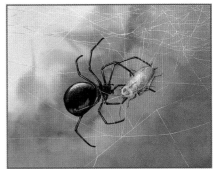

PLATE 7

The Eastern Wood Tick is a parasite that lives by sucking the blood of birds, mammals, and reptiles. The tick clings to plants with its back legs and stretches out its front legs, ready to grab onto an animal. When one passes by, the tick climbs on, attaches itself, and begins to feed. After the tick is full of blood, it drops off.

PLATE 8

Though some scorpions use their poisonous sting to defend themselves or to capture food, many use their front claws instead. Less than 2 percent of the world's scorpions are dangerous to people. Even the Giant Desert Hairy Scorpion, which can grow to 5 1/2 inches in length, is not a threat to humans. It eats mostly insects, but sometimes catches small lizards and snakes.

PLATE 9
Spiders spin silk for many reasons. Probably the most well-known reason is to trap food. Different types of spiders build webs of different shapes. Orb weavers build spiral, circular webs. The Golden Silk Spider's gold-colored web may be 2 to 3 feet across.

PLATE 10
When baby spiders get ready to find a place to live and hunt, they climb onto a branch or a blade of grass and release a few threads of silk. The wind catches the threads and then carries the spiderlings through the air, sometimes for many miles. This is called ballooning. The little Garden Spiders in the picture are traveling in this way.

PLATE 11
Most spiders make cases from silk to protect their eggs. The Nursery Web Spider does not build a web to catch prey, but it does build a nursery web to hold the egg sac as hatching time approaches. The mother spider stays nearby to guard the eggs until they hatch and the spiderlings are ready to move away.

PLATE 12
Some kinds of female spiders die soon after laying their eggs. Some leave their egg sacs, but others stay to guard them. The Rabid Wolf Spider drags her egg sac around until the babies hatch and crawl onto her back.

Like other scorpions, the Sculptured Centruroides Scorpion carries her babies on her back until they shed their exoskeleton for the first time. This is the only scorpion in the U.S. with a sting that may be deadly to people.

PLATE 13

The smallest arachnids are mites. Many mites are parasites, living on other animals or plants. Some chigger mites bite people and cause severe itching. The Velvet Mite eats insect eggs. Even though it is only 1/8 inch long, it is easily recognized by its red color and velvety hair.

PLATE 14

The bite or sting of an arachnid is usually most effective on its prey, but some species are harmful to people. Ticks sometimes spread diseases. Mites may damage crops by sucking the juices from plants. A bite from a Brown Recluse Spider can cause illness and a wound that may take months to heal.

PLATE 15

Arachnids play an important role in keeping nature in balance. Spiders eat insects that humans consider to be pests. The Daring Jumping Spider is often found in homes. These bold spiders have good appetites. One captive individual ate more than forty fruit flies at one sitting.

Cathryn Sill, a former elementary school teacher, is the author of the acclaimed ABOUT... series. With her husband John and her brother-in-law Ben Sill, she coauthored the popular bird-guide parodies, A FIELD GUIDE TO LITTLE-KNOWN AND SELDOM-SEEN BIRDS OF NORTH AMERICA, ANOTHER FIELD GUIDE TO LITTLE-KNOWN AND SELDOM-SEEN BIRDS OF NORTH AMERICA, and BEYOND BIRDWATCHING, all from Peachtree Publishers.

John Sill is a prize-winning and widely published wildlife artist who illustrated the ABOUT... series and coauthored the FIELD GUIDES and BEYOND BIRDWATCHING. A native of North Carolina, he holds a B.S. in Wildlife Biology from North Carolina State University.

The Sills live and work in Franklin, North Carolina.